P9-DHC-263

HURRICANES AND TORNADOES

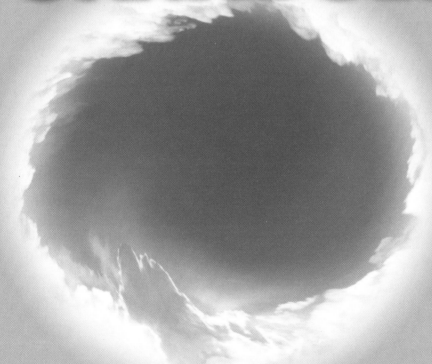

KATE WATERS

SCHOLASTIC INC.

New York   Toronto   London   Auckland   Sydney
Mexico City   New Delhi   Hong Kong   Buenos Aires

ISBN-13: 978-0-545-07229-8
ISBN-10: 0-545-07229-8

12 11 10 9 8 7 6 5 4 3 2   8 9 10 11 12 13/0

Printed in the U.S.A.
First printing, September 2008

Hurricanes and tornadoes are violent storms. Both have very strong winds. These winds spin in circles.

A hurricane forms over the ocean.
This storm is most dangerous when
it moves toward land and hits towns

along the coasts. A hurricane can also
be dangerous to boats that get caught
in it.

Weather scientists, called meteorologists, can tell if a hurricane is forming. They look at photographs of the Earth. These photos are taken from space.

Can you find the hurricane?

From above, a hurricane looks like
a big white circle with a hole in the
center. That circle of clouds is about 300
miles wide. From below, the clouds look
like a dark storm. Strong winds blow.
Heavy rain falls. Huge waves crash.

Most hurricanes happen during the months when the surface of the ocean is very warm. These months are called hurricane season.

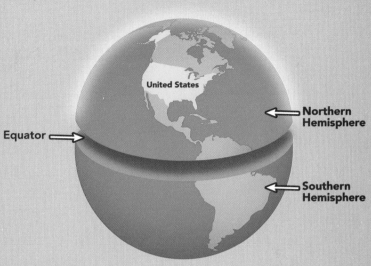

United States

Equator ⟹

Northern
Hemisphere ⟸

Southern
Hemisphere ⟸

Hurricane season lasts
from June to November in
the Northern Hemisphere. It
lasts from November to April
in the Southern Hemisphere.
Hurricanes are called
typhoons in the West Pacific
Ocean and cyclones in the
Indian Ocean and South
Pacific Ocean.

Scientists get information from instruments on special airplanes that fly right into hurricanes. They measure wind speed and mark the location of the storm. Meteorologists collect all this information. They use computers to predict if the hurricane will hit land. They warn people who are in the hurricane's path.

People gather supplies when hurricane season is coming. They protect their houses. They put boards over their windows.

People put away outside objects like chairs and toys. They may be told to leave if the storm is going to be very strong.

It is very dangerous to be outside when a hurricane hits land. The wind can knock trees over and pull walls from houses. The rain falls so heavily that it is hard to see anything. Strong winds push ocean water into huge swells. That water can wash over streets and cars. It can flood houses.

The center of a hurricane has a quiet space. It is called the eye. Some people may think it is safe to go outside in the eye of the storm. But the hurricane is still moving. The second half of the storm is on the way.

Reporters and photographers sometimes try to stay in towns that will be hit by hurricanes. They want to gather facts to share with others. But sometimes it is not safe to stay.

Emergency workers may have to rescue people and pets after a strong hurricane. Then people help each other clean up. They rebuild their communities together.

A tornado forms over land. It can cause a lot of damage to buildings, roads, and people. Tornadoes are smaller storms than hurricanes, but their winds are much stronger.

Tornadoes are created by thunderstorms. They are sometimes called twisters.

Tornadoes have two parts: a storm and a funnel cloud. The storm usually causes thunder, lightning, and rain. The funnel cloud reaches down from the storm to the ground. The wind spins in a circle.

Tornado wind carried this grand piano ¼ mile and dropped it in the middle of a cornfield!

Tornado winds are very strong. Some tornadoes have winds that can blow up to 300 miles an hour! The wind can pick up houses and cattle and trucks. It can even bend thick steel beams. People can get hit by flying objects.

The United States has more tornadoes than any other country. There are more than 1,000 a year. Every state can have tornadoes. But most of them touch down in Tornado Alley. This area includes Texas, Oklahoma, Kansas, Nebraska, and South Dakota. It also includes smaller areas of Iowa and Colorado.

Meteorologists use radar to keep track of big storms. They also count on tornado spotters. These people quickly call the police when they see funnel clouds. Sometimes they take photographs.

People who live where there are many tornadoes have emergency plans. They go to basements or underground tornado shelters. They stay there until the storm has passed. If there is not time, they move away from windows and crawl under desks or benches.

Some tornadoes touch the ground for only two or three minutes. The strongest tornadoes can move across the ground for up to 25 minutes. They leave a path of damage behind them.

Funnel clouds
eventually disappear.
Then people help
each other clean up.
They rebuild houses
and stores.

Dangerous storms are a part of nature. We can't stop them from happening. But we can get ready for them. Knowing how to stay safe during storms can keep us from getting hurt.

Glossary

beam—a long, thick piece of wood, concrete, or metal used to support the roof or floors of a building

emergency—a sudden and dangerous situation that must be dealt with quickly

funnel—a shape like a cone

meteorologist—a person who studies weather

Northern Hemisphere—the half of Earth that is north of the equator

shelter—a place where you can keep covered in bad weather or stay safe and protected from danger

Southern Hemisphere—the half of Earth that is south of the equator

swells—long, rolling waves

violent—powerful